The Pregnancy Guide For Men

The Brand-New, Easy-to-Follow Step-by-Step
Survival Guide for First-Time Fathers: Everything
You Need to Know to Enjoy Every Moment of
Your New Role as a Father While Staying Safe and
Stress-Free

Richard Minner

Contents

your life and not a time of stress and confusion.

Introduction

In today's ever-evolving culture, being a parent is a dynamic role that must adapt to new circumstances. Today, be a reliable and kind father to your children.

What are some of the responsibilities that come along with becoming a father?

Men may be able to assist their children in developing confidence and self-esteem by following the helpful parenting tips shown here, and in doing so, they may discover how to be more involved, supporting, and loving fathers to their own children. The practice of fatherhood is undergoing change with societal norms and the conventional family unit as a whole.

Included in this category are families with a single parent, blended families, families with parents of the same gender, families with multiple generations, and families with parents of different genders.

In the three decades prior, today's fathers will tell you that their interactions with their own fathers were very different from how they interact with their own sons and daughters. This is something that today's fathers will tell you is very different from how they interact with their own sons and daughters.

Because of developments in methods of parenting, it is now much simpler for men to adjust to the responsibilities that come with becoming fathers, spouses, or partners.

It is becoming less common for a parent in today's society to immediately look to his or her own experiences as a child or teenager for guidance regarding parenting.

Chapter 1: Simple tricks and tactics to succeed through pregnancy--and know what to do at each stage of pregnancy.

You can expect a challenging time ahead, but even in the nine months leading up to parenthood, there are also some things you should prepare for. I think it is fair to say that I had a rollercoaster of emotions throughout the process, and I have shared a few reasons why so far. The baby shower, although not essential, is much more commonplace and is worth the experience. Lastly, your lady's body is going to change (no duh), and she is going to get quite physically uncomfortable. Get the massage oils at the ready, put a smile on, and be prepared to listen to, recognize, and respond appropriately to her complaints as you will need to become the source of comfort for her in the next nine months.

When you first find out that your lady is pregnant, you may respond with a mixture of emotions ranging from excitement to dread. I was in disbelief upon hearing the news and almost doubted if it was true until we received confirmation from our healthcare provider. I think part of this was because my wife got pregnant as soon as we started trying. I actually expected that it would take us a bit longer as it does with most couples, but I suppose we are extremely fortunate not to have this problem. Throughout the pregnancy, when people asked me how I felt, I would often respond that I was just as thrilled and terrified. I was ready to be a father, but at the same time, I was not, and I was fearful that I would not be able to do it. I was enthusiastic and anxious.

I did not know what the hell I was supposed to do to take care of a baby. My exposure to such responsibilities was limited to holding my nieces or nephews for a few minutes until they started to fuss, then I would pass them off to their parents. Luckily for me, my wife is a pediatrician and has considerable babysitting and childcare experience; so, I followed her lead. Still, I could not help but feel somewhat helpless as the delivery date drew closer. It is such a thrilling time, but scary. I do not believe that I am alone in feeling this way, as some of my friends who are first-time dads said they had the same feelings, as did some of my relatives when they were about to have their first child. This is to say that it is reasonable to expect to have this same fear, and there is no shame in admitting it. The excitement will prevail, however; as our due date drew near, I counted down the days and crossed off the hurdles (such as work responsibilities and graduate school projects) until there was nothing left to do but wait for the induction date or for labor to begin naturally.

Looking back now, I somewhat miss the anticipation of the delivery and being able to meet my son for the first time. I will go into my experience of the delivery in Part II, but I think one thing that did worry me were the many complications that could occur during delivery. This fear was partially due to my wife's exposure to many horribly sad deliveries that she had to attend as a resident physician during her rotations in labor and delivery. Some seemingly perfect pregnancies (and completely healthy fetuses) followed by an unexpected difficult delivery resulted in some babies either dying or experiencing such trauma to the point that they would never be able to live a normal life. It is important to point out that my wife was exposed to a large sample size of deliveries, so she was bound to be present for more complications as a result, and would then share those sad, and scary experiences with me. Although you should recognize that deliveries are intense – and they absolutely are – women have been giving birth for thousands of years, and medicine has been aggressively improving every year to continually improve outcomes.

Be excited for this next stage of your life, and some things are worth worrying about, but do not let that fear overcome you.

We decided to have a baby shower after my mother-in-law convinced my wife to do it. My wife didn't really want to have one, because it seemed to be yet another expense that we'd have to deal with. In her words, it seemed like we were paying for another (albeit cheaper) wedding reception. I know some people who have not had a baby shower, and that is absolutely fine, too. You should not feel pressured either way, but after my experience, I am glad that we decided to go for it. We chose a rather well-known Mexican restaurant near our home to host our baby shower, because 1) it was reasonably priced, 2) we would not have to travel all that far, and we did not have enough room in our home to host it, and 3) we like Mexican food and tequila (although my wife was unable to enjoy the latter on that day). We decided to make our baby shower coed, although I know some women prefer to only invite women to it. You and your lady should decide that which will work best for you.

There are pros and cons of having the baby shower. Of course, it can be a headache to plan it all and invite everyone whom you want to attend. She invited many of her friends who lived in the same city as us at the time, and I was friends with many of their husbands, so I actually enjoyed the experience. Our baby shower occurred during the last few weeks of the NFL season, so some of the guys and I were ripping tequila shots and streaming games from our phones while the ladies played some of the common baby shower games (e.g., guess the due date, baby weight and length, etc.). It was a good time. My wife and I had made a registry, but before we filled it out, we spoke to my sisters, sisters-in-law, and mothers about what we should have on our registry. There are so many things that can be put on your registry that you will never use. If you do not know if something is worth including, I would highly recommend that you spend time with someone who has been through the process several times to refine your list to ensure you only have what you deem as the most essential. We did find that although hosting the baby shower did cost us some money (booking the room and buying the food and drink), we actually came out on top considering the value of all of the gifts that we were given. Again – it was stuff we would have had to purchase anyway, like diapers, wipes, etc., so we found it was absolutely worth the time and expense. You should not take this as me saying that you need to have a baby shower, nor am I saying that you need not have a baby shower. In my experience, it worked out well, but I recognize that may not be the case for everyone. However, I will say that unwrapping the many boxes of diapers did start to make it more real for me, as did my wife's growing belly. Our little dude was going to be arriving soon.

Watching the pregnant belly slowly grow over nine months is truly remarkable. My wife and I look back on pictures she took of herself from various stages of the pregnancy, and the difference between when she first started to show her baby bump to the last picture we took at the hospital before she was induced. It was incredible. It should come as no surprise that as the pregnancy progresses, your lady will become increasingly more uncomfortable. Her daily routine will start to be impacted in ways that you simply cannot relate. Take sleeping, for example: after many months of pregnancy, my wife could not find a comfortable position. She normally likes to sleep on her belly, but that is out of the question during pregnancy. She ordered some large pregnancy pillows to help, and they did help a bit, but it did not make a considerable difference. If this means that you have a little less room on the bed to sleep at night, suck it up. You really do not have any space to complain to someone who is growing a human inside of their body. Keep that in perspective throughout pregnancy – you simply cannot relate to what she is going through. It may be difficult for her to find a comfortable position in which to sit on the couch. Can you imagine your body changing so quickly to the point that you cannot sit comfortably? It is difficult for me to relate to that.

On a more intimate note, some women find it difficult to get in a comfortable position to do the no-pants dance. I know my wife found this positioning to be difficult, even if she still enjoyed the sex itself. She said that she felt disgusted when we tried, but obviously, I did not think so – nor would I care. For some women, pregnancy hormones can cause them to get crazily horny. That was not the experience that my wife had, but it is certainly possible. I really envy the guys whose ladies do experience that.

Your lady is going to start feeling larger every day; in my wife's words, she said she felt like a beached whale. If humor is a big part of your relationship – as it is for us – then go ahead and try to crack a joke at her expense. However, always remember that the pregnancy hormones are powerful, so tread lightly. As the pregnancy progresses, her legs and feet will begin to swell, her back will become sore, and she may get terrible heartburn. My wife's heartburn was so bad that it would wake her up in the middle of the night, and she would not be able to fall back asleep, though this may have also been due to an inability to find a comfortable sleeping position. It certainly is not a bad idea to surprise her with a nice pair of compression socks, offer to give her a back rub whenever she wants, and have a bottle of famotidine handy to proactively prevent heartburn. You should be ready to be at her beck and call because she will be going through somewhat of a miserable experience. I do not believe that I have met any woman who has said that they had "fun" being pregnant. It is a life-changing experience, for sure, but I am pretty sure every woman who is pregnant cannot wait to be done being pregnant by the end of the third trimester.

Remember to keep things in perspective and recognize that your lady is going through a lengthy and rather traumatic experience. You really should not have much to complain about, and if you do, keep it to yourself; she's going through a lot already. She is not going to feel bad for you. When my mother-in-law was giving birth to my wife, she experienced a very difficult, long labor. After some time, and while my mother-in-law was still pushing, my father-in-law mentioned that his back hurt from standing for so long. I would advise against doing this. It did not end well.

You should try to understand why your lady would not want to go to an event (e.g., a concert), a friend's house, or a bar. She is going to be more comfortable at home, and it is not like she can enjoy alcohol if you decide to have a night on the town. She is simply not going to have the same experience as you are. There may also be times that pregnancy gets her down, or it may simply frustrate her that she would not be able to do something as easy as sitting comfortably on the couch. Remind her of how amazing it is for a human being to be forming in her. She often says to me, "isn't it crazy that we made him?" Yes, it is, although she did the lion's share of the work. Sure, I played a role in the procreation process, but that role was easy. I did not have to cook him inside of me for nine months.

Chapter 2: Importance of a birth plan and how to organize one

Once you have made it through conception to the point of your partner getting pregnant, whether it was a quick and easy process or a lengthy and difficult one, there are a whole host of new issues to face. But first – congratulations! You are now expecting a child. You and your partner are likely experiencing all kinds of emotions, including excitement, exhaustion, and anxiety.

This chapter educates you on things you need to consider at the very beginning of pregnancy and how you can support your partner through all the initial symptoms, emotions, and decisions.

Chapter 3: Notions divided into three trimesters and month by month, from the pregnancy test to when the baby will be home, and information on what to expect and what you need to do after the birth

Testing for Confirmation

As soon as she missed a period or even displayed the slightest early pregnancy symptom, your partner probably raced off to the nearest pharmacy. Over-the-counter pregnancy tests can sometimes give inaccurate results, but they are more likely to give a false negative result than a false positive result. Testing the first-morning urine can improve accuracy because it is more concentrated at this time. Even if you have a positive result from an at-home test, the first thing you want to do is get confirmation from a doctor.

Make an appointment with a family doctor or obstetrician, who will test your partner's urine for the hormone human chorionic gonadotropin (HCG). HCG is the hormone responsible for the morning sickness and utter exhaustion your other half has to look forward to if she isn't already experiencing these symptoms. The doctor may also perform a gynecological exam on your partner to check the physical signs of pregnancy more closely. She may also have to go to the lab for a blood test to determine the exact level HCG in the blood. A blood test will help pinpoint how far along into the pregnancy she is.

Even your doctor can only provide a definitive answer when the pregnancy symptoms are apparent, which is around four weeks after fertilization. So, you should probably wait a little while before you start telling everyone the good news. You may want to wait awhile, until after the first ultrasound scan. We'll talk more about that in the next chapter. For now, keep this incredible news between the two of you.

Once you have confirmed the pregnancy, a celebration with your partner is in order! Treat her to a romantic evening at home or out on the town, depending on how she is feeling. Just remember that cigarettes, alcohol, and drugs are off the menu.

Second trimester

It's a terrific idea to consider ways to strengthen your marriage throughout the second trimester.

You should seek professional assistance if you or your partner are going through emotional upheavals that continue longer than two weeks and interfere with your daily life.

Many couples find that their relationship has stabilized during the second trimester. During these months, the chance of miscarriage is greatly reduced. In most cases, morning sickness ends between 14 and 16 weeks. Changes in her body and hormones may lead her desire for sex to change, and her attitude and energy will undoubtedly improve.

Throughout the second trimester, there are a few things to consider.

Now is the time to consider and discuss significant issues like starting a family, money, wills, and strengthening your relationship. Pregnancy-related open communication can set the way for a later-life parenting connection that is beneficial and successful. Therefore, talking to your partner about any changes in your relationship may make you feel more at ease. This holds true regardless of your worries regarding your finances or other aspects of your relationship.

Now that morning sickness is likely behind, the second trimester is a good time to concentrate on healthy food and exercise.

You could start to reflect about what it means to be a father. Maybe you've already started thinking about the activities you'd like to undertake with your kid and are excited to be their teacher and mentor.

Second trimester food cravings

You need to keep an eye out for strange and delectable food desires. Will your companion wake up in the morning yearning ice cream and hummus? Or do you enjoy cereal as a snack before bed?

But don't be shocked if your friend simply eats a little bit more frequently and without any apparent urges.

There are other things that occur during pregnancy besides mood swings.

Changes in your partner's mood are more likely to stabilize towards the middle of the year.

If you observe a significant change in your partner's or your own mood and behavior, you may need to seek therapy for depression, anxiety, stress, or other mood disorders. If you or your partner are enduring mood or emotional changes that last more than two weeks and are affecting daily living, it's time to see a doctor.

Do something enjoyable together with your partner to strengthen your bond.

Talk to your partner about any changes in your relationship. Be understanding and honest with one another about the range of emotions you're feeling.

Talk to your partner about finances, household responsibilities (such as who does what), and anything else that comes to mind.

Do you have a living trust or a will? Is this the most recent update? Have you purchased life insurance? It's a great chance to take care of these important issues.

Pregnancy in the middle

The second trimester sees an increase in sex and sexual desire.

You can have sex if your pregnancy is developing normally.

Sexual desire changes are common. In the second trimester, your husband can be more or less interested in having sex.

If you do engage in sexual activity, let your partner decide on a comfortable position.

The general consensus is that as long as everything is going well and you and your partner are both interested, having sex while pregnant is acceptable. On the other hand, most men discover that they have less possibilities for sex when a woman is expecting a child.

Sex may feel very differently during pregnancy than it did beforehand. You can also worry that the child will suffer sexual injury. Since your child is protected and enclosed in the amniotic sac, you cannot harm him or her during sexual activity.

Visit your doctor, midwife, or obstetrician if you have any queries or concerns, such as if your partner is bleeding while pregnant. They'll tell you if having sex is acceptable.

Your spouse can be more animated and eager for sex during the pregnancy.

Early pregnancy signs like nausea, exhaustion, and breast tenderness are probably gone by now. Hormones and increased blood flow to her genitals may make orgasming simpler for her.

Additionally, it's natural for your spouse to become less interested in having sex throughout the second trimester.

The form of your partner's body will change. Let her pick a comfortable sexual position for you if you do engage in sex.

If your doctor has advised against having sex or if neither of you desire to have sex, you and your partner can still remain close. You can still kiss, embrace, cuddle, or massage each other, for instance.

Try to prioritize your partner's needs and keep her feelings in mind. If she is still experiencing nausea, vomiting, bloating, and painful breasts, she might not want to have sex.

It may be helpful to discuss any sexual frustrations with your partner so that you are both aware of what is happening.

It's advised to exercise lightly.

When pregnant, light to moderate exercise is typically safe. Pregnant women who are physically active can handle the challenges of pregnancy and delivery better. Changes in your partner's weight and shape could endanger her balance and coordination as early as the second trimester. Working out with your spouse could motivate her to maintain her fitness.

Healthy pregnant women with straightforward pregnancies can continue to engage in regular, moderate exercise after consulting their midwives, general practitioners, or obstetricians.

Start a light-to-moderate workout program when pregnant. Why is it crucial to stay physically active when pregnant? There are several advantages to staying active throughout pregnancy for both the mother and the unborn child.

Women who engage in 30 minutes of moderate aerobic exercise a few times per week will feel better overall during their pregnancy. This is because exercise has been shown to reduce back pain and increase energy while also enhancing mood, fitness, and sleep.

Pregnancy-related physical activity may lower your partner's risk of pre-eclampsia, gestational diabetes, and excessive weight gain. She might find it easier to manage the delivery procedure as a result.

A fantastic method for you to strengthen your relationship and create a "team" that will support you once the kid is born is to exercise together. In the second trimester, combining walking and swimming is a fantastic exercise option.

After having a kid, men's levels of physical activity typically decrease. If you and your spouse establish some healthy routines now, you may be more likely to stay active following the birth of your child.

Your partner's baby bulge steadily grows during the second trimester. From now until delivery, your partner's body weight and form may change, which could endanger her balance and coordination. She might find some activities unpleasant.

Changes in blood pressure starting in the fourth month suggest that your spouse should refrain from making abrupt position changes, including from from lying down to standing up. This will make her feel less lightheaded.

Going for a stroll is one of the most effective ways to exercise. And you can still invite your walking companion to join you. You won't have as much couple time after the birth of your child.

We can now spend time together, which is good.

You might be able to convince your companion to accompany you on a 30-minute walk. Start with three days per week and work your way up to five. If you're used to more demanding activities, like running, think of the walk as a warm-up before going for a run on your own.

You should be able to continue taking regular walks as part of your training plan even after the baby is delivered. Avoid walking or engaging in other forms of exercise during the hottest parts of the day to keep your spouse safe and healthy. Make certain she also receives adequate water.

Until a health professional advises otherwise, encourage your partner to exercise.

Maintain an active lifestyle to help you stay energized while you get ready for the birth of your child.

Take your companion for a stroll. You and your partner can use it to be active both before and after the baby is born.

Think about going swimming with a pal. It's a fantastic way to work out, especially when your partner's "bump" grows larger.

Late Pregnancy in the third Trimester

Late in pregnancy is the best time to start preparing for your responsibilities as a birth supporter and your first moments as a father.

Attend birth classes, prenatal exams, and hospital visits as much as you can, and consider making changes at work.

Your partner can experience anxiety throughout the third trimester. Talking to her about how you can assist her is a smart idea.

Being a father can feel very real to you right now or it might not.

What takes place during a pregnancy's third trimester?

Both the mother and the unborn child have undergone additional medical examinations in the recent months. If you and your partner can coordinate these appointments, that's excellent. A fetal doppler's ability to detect your unborn child's heartbeat can be both thrilling and comforting.

Your youngster can hear both you and your partner. Start speaking to the infant or singing some of your favorite songs if you haven't already.

Your doctor or midwife will assess the baby's posture as your due date draws near to determine whether the child is prepared to be born head-down. If your baby is in an uncommon position, your doctor or midwife will talk to you about your options.

As the baby grows and moves more, your spouse is probably going to feel more uncomfortable. This could have an impact on how excited you and your partner are to have sex at the end of your pregnancy. As your partner uses pillows and searches for ways to sleep comfortably, your portion of the bed may seem to shrink with time.

As soon as the baby goes to sleep, your spouse might wake up needing to use the restroom since the baby is pressing on her bladder. For those nights when your baby need multiple feedings, think of it as a form of early training.

Your companion can express complaints of a hurting back, exhaustion, heartburn, agitation, or lack of sleep. This is probably not going to stop her from "nesting," which could involve organizing and cleaning your house in preparation for the baby's arrival.

Planning should start during the third trimester.

In the third trimester and in the initial hours following delivery, you should begin to consider your position as a birth supporter.

It's a good idea to consider and read about how to start off as a good parent in the weeks and months following the birth of your child. Many parents focus solely on the birth of their child and ignore what happens after that.

It's a good idea to take birthing classes, speak with other guys who are pregnant or just became fathers, and tour the hospital where your child will be delivered.

Consider your career and any changes you might want to make, such as negotiating parental leave or reassessing your work-life balance, throughout your late pregnancy. If you get the chance, talk with your manager about the ideal setup for you. However, as your thoughts or feelings could change, remain adaptable in your plans.

Accepting or requesting practical assistance from family and friends is another fantastic method to get ready. Practical help may provide you and your partner more time to focus on your child and rest after your baby is delivered. This could involve cooking, cleaning, grocery shopping, or driving.

You can talk or sing to your child; they will hear you.

Discuss with your partner how you might support her in feeling more at ease and obtaining more sleep.

Attend classes on childbirth education. Ask your students what they are doing to get ready for the birth of their children: are they reading books, watching births on the internet, using breathing and relaxation techniques, or helping to create a birth plan?

Make plans to attend the hospital where your partner will give birth, if at all possible.

Talk to your spouse about how you feel about having children. It's acceptable to experience fear or uncertainty.

If you are aware of any other dads' children, ask about their births.

Consult your doctor or midwife if you have any questions or concerns regarding anything pertaining to the delivery or the health of your child.

See if your employer will be willing to allow you time off for childbirth and recovery by asking them.

Invite friends and relatives to aid you before the birth of your child.

It is impossible to emphasize the value of prenatal care.

You might need to inform your doctor that you wish to participate more actively in your prenatal care.

If you introduce yourself and be friendly and courteous, you are more likely to be welcomed.

You might find it easier to focus on your talks with medical professionals if you have a list of questions.

Midwives and obstetricians used to focus solely on mothers and young children. Hospitals and other birthing facilities are becoming increasingly mindful of the desire of partners to participate in the pregnancy, childbirth, and upbringing of their children.

Healthcare professionals are working harder to engage with guys, and male-only birth classes are becoming increasingly prevalent. These are indications that prenatal treatment for males who are expecting children is becoming more prevalent in hospitals.

If you wish to be more actively involved in your pregnancy, prenatal care, and delivery, midwife-led antenatal care may be a fantastic option. You and your spouse will come to know the same midwife or a small group of midwives over your pregnancy. Many of these initiatives allow visits outside of regular business hours to make participation easier for partners.

Appointment times are usually constrained, and hospital employees are frequently overworked. Staff members may not genuinely care if they don't inquire about your well-being. They can be looking into a variety of issues with your spouse and unborn child.

Some employees are more adept at involving males than others. It will be up to you to express your desire to participate in the discussion as well as any occasional reservations you might have.

You'll have a better chance of joining the conversation if you make an effort to introduce yourself and are cordial and pleasant. It's also a good idea to be on time and turn off your phone to avoid disturbing people. This makes it quite evident that this appointment is the top priority on your mind right now.

It will be simpler to focus your talks with healthcare professionals if you have a list of questions. If you're pressed for time, you can ask your closest friends or family right away. Do not be afraid to make "stupid" inquiries. It is a good idea to inquire if you are uncertain of what is happening.

Attend your prenatal visits on time, put your phone away, say hello, and act politely and amiably.

Bring a list of any inquiries you may have for medical professionals to your appointments.

Inform the doctor or a staff member that you would like to participate if you feel excluded. Aim for a balance between letting them concentrate on the infant and interrogating them.

Third trimester sexual activity

You might worry more about sexually abusing your unborn child in the final trimesters of your pregnancy. Since your child is protected and enclosed in the amniotic sac, you cannot harm him or her during sexual activity.

Sex in the later months is acceptable if the pregnancy is going smoothly and both you and your partner are ready. However, most men claim to have less sex as the pregnancy goes on.

If your doctor has advised against having sex or if neither of you desire to have sex, you and your partner can still remain close. You can still kiss, embrace, cuddle, or massage each other, for instance.

Physical difficulties can occur when having sex with a pregnant partner. You might need to get inventive and attempt various sexual positions as her stomach grows. She can be too huge and unpleasant to have sex with if she is expecting twins, triplets, or more. Another factor contributing to women's lack of sex readiness at this stage of pregnancy is the fact that they are typically exhausted. Your sweetheart probably isn't as lovely as they ought to be. And you might discover that no amount of flattery or kind words can make her feel better or arouse her desire for sex.

Finding sex has been nearly difficult. She demanded a lot of sex after eight weeks throughout the following four months, according to a friend. I didn't have sex the entire time my wife was pregnant, another man alleged. It's all a part of the process, I suppose. I have to acknowledge that things are as they are in reality. It won't last indefinitely.

Explore sexual positions that are enjoyable and comfortable for your spouse, following her direction.

Try to prioritize your partner's needs and keep her feelings in mind. She might be experiencing discomfort at this point in her pregnancy.

It's a good idea to talk to your spouse about any sexual problems you're having so that both of you can understand what the other is going through.

Wait a bit longer; although it may be annoying, the inability to have sex with your husband won't last forever.

At the time, massages of her feet, legs, and lower back among other things were the only thing that drew us closer. My wife was quite appreciative. Men don't often consider this, but it's awful to be unable to touch your own toes. I believe that men should always assist women because they go through a lot of pain. The state of being pregnant is transient.

Chapter 4: Do's and don'ts of planning a family with your partner.

Things to Do to Celebrate and Start Preparing

Your life will change drastically in just nine months. The best time to do some things with your partner that might not be possible when your baby is born is right now. You might think about doing the following activities to mark your impending parenthood, spend time with your partner, and be ready:

• Since your spouse is already pregnant, indulge in loads of unprotected sex. Always be sensitive to her moods because she can be too unwell, worn out, or overwhelmed for sex.

• Go on a romantic getaway with your significant other. Make the most of your vacation while you can because it won't be like this for around 18 years.

• Consider how you experienced growing up and what you want your child to know.

• Take a late night, prepare brunch for you and your spouse, or go on a picnic with them.

• Indulge in a date night at a posh restaurant or a day at the spa.

• Create a notebook, blog, or scrapbook to record the months leading up to the birth of your kid. You can give it to your child as a keepsake when she is older. This sentimental gesture from you will move and please your partner!

• Then practice on your spouse after learning how to massage. Even a few high-quality aromatherapy oils are available. Over the next nine months, she will be very grateful for your efforts!

• Schedule regular check-ins with your spouse and talk about how you both are feeling. How can you assist? When she expresses thoughts, hopes, or anxieties, be open to hearing them. Avoid the desire to "fix" anything unless she specifically requests assistance. She'll be aware of your efforts and appreciative given that she presumably has a range of emotions right now.

Chapter Five

Chapter 5: Common mistakes

Every parent errs occasionally. You don't think so? One of the hardest jobs you'll ever have is being a parent, especially the first few months when your baby is a newborn. Parenting is a learning process where you make errors and eventually become an expert. But by simply being aware of several frequent mistakes, you may really make the entire process simple and less stressful.

Here are some errors that new parents frequently make, along with advice on how to avoid them:

First new-parent error: worrying excessively about everything

Panicking over everything is the biggest error that new parents make. During the first few years of parenthood, parents worry a lot about little things. The baby's diet, sleep, and crying worry parents. Therefore, if you are one of those parents who is constantly in a state of panic, stop worrying about everything. You and your baby won't benefit from worrying unnecessarily. Instead, keep your cool, take your child to the doctor frequently, and ask the professionals to clarify any questions or concerns you may have.

The second rookie parenting error is not letting your child cry it out.

When your kid cries nonstop, do you worry? Let's go! We are familiar with you... Your infant is sobbing, and you are baffled as to why. If your infant is crying uncontrollably, it's okay. Being a baby involves crying. Your baby is well known to you. If you suspect a problem, consult your doctor right away. Call your doctor for assistance if your infant is experiencing fever, rash, vomiting, or a swollen belly while sobbing uncontrollably.

Third rookie error: Ignoring fever

Parents frequently believe that their child's temperature of 100.4 is normal and that with home treatment, their child would quickly recover. However, it is an emergency if a newborn under 3 months old has a temperature of 100.4 or higher. Don't take chances if your infant has a temperature. It is preferable that you see a doctor. The immune system of a newborn cannot effectively combat numerous illnesses. Seek for medical help as soon as you can.

Fourth rookie error: waking the infant to breastfeed.

It is true that a baby's best source of nutrients is breast milk. The infant must only consume the mother's milk for the next six months. However, that does not entail that you must feed your sleeping newborn every two to three hours. A well-breasted infant should snooze peacefully all night long.

To learn more: Wintertime Activities for Toddlers

The fifth rookie error involves neglecting dental hygiene.

Infant oral care is sometimes neglected by new parents until it is too late. For newborns as for adults, oral hygiene is crucial. Therefore, the next time you feed your baby, be sure to clean his or her gums with a soft, wet towel. Allow your baby to sip on some water after feedings since the fluoride in water helps prevent cavities.

Sixth rookie parenting error: failing to share your labor

Keep your spouse involved in splitting the job. Let the infant discover his own path even if he isn't the best at bathing and feeding him. Together with your partner, split up the baby's duties. Together, you'll accomplish more and have less work to do while growing closer.

The seventh rookie error is ignoring your spouse.

Because of the new family member, you could get so preoccupied that you neglect your spouse (especially women). You must prioritize your relationship with your partner, though. Assure him that you have quality time with him. Go out for a dinner date with your partner while leaving your infant with your in-laws or parents. It will support maintaining the passion in your marriage.

The eighth rookie error is fighting excessively (or insufficiently) in front of your child.

Does your infant witness your arguments or fights? Never do it. Fighting and bickering can harm a baby's brain development. Their extremely responsive brain might be negatively impacted by any type of fighting or abuse.

9th rookie error: the infant talks

Hearing your infant coo and babble is blissful. However, it's possible that your tiny one will begin absorbing language far sooner than you think. Therefore, be careful not to mislead your newborn with baby babble. Speak to the child in an infant-directed manner. With simple-to-understand facial expressions and brief, precise instructions, you may easily draw someone's attention.

Trusting dubious sources for parenting guidance is the tenth rookie error for parents.

Your neighbor advises allowing the infant to thumb-suck. And you concur with it? The most frequent error made by brand-new parents is choosing the incorrect sources for parenting assistance. Although you must acknowledge their concern for you and your child, only professionals should be relied upon for parenting guidance. You may always consult a professional for parenting-related issues, or you can browse the internet for information about new parenting.

Don't berate yourself for making mistakes; remember, all parents occasionally do so. Just trust your gut and seek out knowledge when you require it.

Chapter Six

Chapter 6: Physical intimacy during pregnancy.

The guiding principle for having sex when pregnant is that as long as both you and your partner are eager and the pregnancy is going well, you can. However, the majority of men find that they have less sex when they are expecting a child.

Pregnancy might cause sex to feel significantly different from how it did before. You could worry that having sex would harm the unborn child. You cannot harm your unborn child by engaging in sexual activity since the amniotic sac walls off and safely protects your child.

Consult your GP, midwife, or obstetrician if you have any questions or encounter any problems, such as your spouse bleeding a little while pregnant. They'll let you know if having sex is acceptable.

Pregnancy sex: the first three months.

Early on, you might come to the conclusion that your partner doesn't enjoy sex at all when they're sick, tired, or both. It could be easier to comprehend why your partner might not be as interested in sex if you try to imagine how she feels physically. Your spouse might not feel up to it for a variety of reasons, including sore breasts and bloating.

More massage and less sex.

If you and your partner have regular intercourse and this abruptly ceases or reduces during pregnancy, you might feel unhappy or angry. You might also just accept it.

In any case, the objective is to focus on improving your relationship rather than letting your sexual grumpiness rule you.

If a health professional has advised against having sex with your husband or if neither of you feels like having sex, you may be close in other ways. You can still kiss, embrace, cuddle, or massage each other, for instance.

A good connection with your partner should include appropriate amounts of sex. However, is it acceptable for you to have sex with your spouse while she is expecting? Yes, most women find that having sex while pregnant is safe. But before you do, both of you should consult your doctor.

The most important information about having sex while pregnant is listed here.

You are permitted to have sex with her if the pregnancy is healthy. You and your partner can adopt comfortable and safe positions when you are pregnant.

Your child is not damaged by sex. While you two are having intercourse, the baby is protected by the amniotic fluid in her uterus.

Having sex while pregnant may not be safe if the woman is experiencing pregnancy problems or has in the past.

After having intercourse with her, if she begins to have painful cramps, heavy bleeding, or begins to leak amniotic fluid, call your doctor or go to the emergency room.

It's acceptable for her sex preferences to have evolved throughout her pregnancy. Recognize your partner and consent to her comfort levels.

When is it unsafe to have sex while pregnant?

To find out if it is okay to have sex with your partner, first consult your doctor. Additionally, it is advised to refrain from having sex while pregnant if she has gone through any of the following.

numerous pregnancies (twins, triplets, or more).

had a miscarriage in the past or is at risk for experiencing one during this pregnancy.

She either had a premature baby in the past or is showing signs of preterm labor now. A preterm birth occurs before 37 weeks of pregnancy, and is referred to as such. Preterm labor is when your period starts before you've been pregnant for 37 whole weeks.

Her cervix is ineffective. When the cervix opens too early in pregnancy, this happens. The cervix, which is located at the top of the vagina, is the opening to the uterus (womb). You might experience early labor as a result of an ineffective cervix.

Placenta previa affects her. This occurs when the placenta completely or partially covers the cervix and descends very low in the uterus. Later in the pregnancy, placenta previa may result in substantial bleeding and other problems.

How can you make sexual activity safe when pregnant?

During pregnancy, sex has no impact on your unborn child. Your child is protected by the uterine muscles and the amniotic fluid that surrounds him or her. The mucus plug helps to prevent infection in your baby. A mass of mucus called the mucous plug prevents the cervix from entering. During sexual activity, watch out that your penis doesn't touch your infant.

Discuss any prohibited sexual behaviors with your healthcare physician. She might be counseled to cut back on her sexual activity in some circumstances or to pay attention to whether she is having contractions after sex.

Even though most pregnant women can have sex without it harming their unborn child, you should still take precautions to protect your child from any viruses you might contract during sex. What you can do to assist keep you and your child safe is as follows:

Make sure your spouse has sex-transmission-infection protection (sometimes termed STIs, sexually transmitted illnesses or STDs, sexually transmitted diseases). An STI is an infection that you can get from unprotected sexual activity or close physical contact with an infected person. STIs may cause problems for the developing fetus throughout pregnancy and childbirth. An STI can be acquired during oral, anal, or vaginal sex. If you have sex when pregnant, make sure it's just you and your wife, and check to see if you don't have any STIs. Be dependable. Avoid having intercourse with someone who might be carrying a STI.

Make sure not to blow air into your partner's vagina if you are having oral sex. Sex that involves both the mouth and genitalia is known as oral sex (sex organs, such as the penis and vagina). An air embolism could develop if you blow into your vagina (an air bubble that blocks a blood vessel). For your spouse and infant, this might present serious challenges.

Find out with your doctor if anal sex is permitted. Anal sex refers to sexual activity involving the penis and the anus. Due to the anus's abundance of bacteria, anal sex might be harmful during pregnancy. Your partner may be more susceptible to developing a vaginal infection if you engage in vaginal contact with her after anal sex. Bacteria are tiny organisms that live within and on the surface of the body. Some microbes are beneficial to the body. But some people could harm you.

What signs or symptoms might there be during or following sex?

Inform your doctor if your partner feels discomfort during sex. Contact your doctor or go to the emergency room if she feels severe bleeding, such as menstrual period flow, amniotic fluid spilling, or excruciating cramps that persist after sexual activity.

While she is pregnant, it is normal to have mild cramps or spotting following sexual activity. Cramping can happen during an orgasm. Mild bleeding is called spotting. She will have a few drips of blood on her underwear when it happens. The spotting is so minor that a panty liner is not covered with blood.

How might becoming pregnant impact your spouse's sexual life?

Her sex drive, often known as her interest in and desire for sex, may change throughout pregnancy. Your sex drive may change due to her body's varying hormone levels, other physical changes, and other factors.

The urge for sex in your partner's life may change. Your partner may occasionally feel more attached to you and occasionally worry more about her health and the welfare of your child. It could be beneficial to openly discuss your worries with your spouse.

Here are some typical changes to sex drive that she might experience when pregnant.

First trimester: The early changes in her body's structure and hormone levels may make her feel gorgeous. However, these modifications may also be a factor in the pregnancy discomforts that make women less enthusiastic in sex, such as weariness or nauseousness, aching breasts, and a need to use the restroom frequently.

Second trimester: She might experience an improvement in her health. She might no longer be bothered by first trimester discomforts, or she might be able to bear them more easily in the second trimester. Although her tummy is growing, it is still small enough for comfortable intercourse. She might desire sex more frequently than in the past!

During pregnancy, women's blood weight increases by about 3 pounds, with the majority of that blood flowing below the waist. She may even be able to have many orgasms due to the increased blood flow.

Third trimester: Unless your healthcare professional has advised you differently, you and your partner are free to engage in sexual activity up until the delivery of your child. Your partner can become less eager for sex as the pregnancy comes to an end. She could find certain sex positions uncomfortable as her belly gets bigger. Given that she is more concerned with getting pregnant and having a new baby, she might even be less interested in having sex. It's acceptable to feel these emotions! Even if you don't want to have sex, you and your partner may still feel loving and connected.

Which sexual positions are most suitable while pregnant?

Positions that are comfortable and helpful early on in pregnancy may become uncomfortable or even hazardous as the pregnancy progresses. For instance, during the fourth month of pregnancy, lying flat on your back (also known as the missionary position) exerts stress on major blood arteries due to the weight of the growing baby. Instead, try these positions:

The winner is your husband. She can control how swift, slow, and at ease she is during sex by adopting this position. It might also make her stomach feel less stressed.

Spooning. With your companion lying behind you, lie sideways. The strain placed on her stomach is lessened when having sex in this posture.

On their hands and knees, your spouse. She has the option of standing up straight using her elbows. Because it relieves pressure on her abdomen, this position is most effective in the first and second trimesters. She might not like this posture when her stomach grows.

What other means of intimacy do you have with your partner?

To show your spouse affection, you don't need to have sex. You could get close by:

Cuddling\Kissing\Massage. You and your partner can now gently massage each other's bodies.

exchange of nakedness. You and your partner touch each other at this point to induce orgasm.

Verbal sex.

Openly and tenderly express your desires to your spouse if you want to stay connected. Let comfort and joy be your guides. Adjust what you're doing if anything doesn't seem right to either of you. Inform your doctor if you have any concerns about how the pregnancy is affecting your marriage.

How soon after giving birth can you have sex with your partner?

It's best to hold off on having sex again until after her postpartum checkup, which will be about 6 weeks after giving birth. When you're both ready to resume having sex, use birth control. Consult your doctor about the best time to begin birth control and which type is safe to use if she is still nursing.

These regular changes may affect her sex life (and yours as well), even after her body has healed:

Changes in hormones may cause her vagina to feel dry, especially if she is breastfeeding. To assist in making the vagina more slippery, apply a lubricating cream or gel. To help her feel more at ease, experiment with different positions.

Her vaginal muscles may be weak after giving birth, which could reduce the amount of pleasure she experiences during intercourse. In most cases, this issue gets better with time. She could strengthen her vaginal muscles by performing Kegel exercises.

She might initially have less sex desire than normal. This might be brought on by hormonal changes following childbirth. So don't be too harsh on her—this is natural. She may not be as interested in sex for a variety of reasons, such as fatigue or stress from caring for her child.

She might have weariness from caring for your newborn. After your baby has dozed off, you and your partner may wish to get some rest. Since you have less time, energy, and focus for sex now that you are a parent, you can also lose interest right immediately.

When you're focused on taking care of a new baby, it could be difficult to take care of yourself! Eat well-balanced meals, stay active every day, and try to relax as much as you can to make you both feel better.

Speak to your partner if you're hesitant to engage in sexual activity once more. There's a chance that your partner will feel similar emotions. If you and your partner want to have sex, try to choose an unpressured time, such as when your child is sound asleep. Intimacy can also be expressed by hugging or kissing your partner.

Within the first year of their child's life, the majority of couples resume their active sex life. Notify your doctor if you're still nervous, have pain or discomfort before starting to have sex, or feel stressed about it.

Actions you can take.

Try to prioritize your partner's needs and keep her feelings in mind. Due to nausea, vomiting, bloating, and aching breasts, she might not feel like engaging in sexual activity.

It could be beneficial to discuss any sexual unhappiness with your partner so that you both understand what the other is going through.

Be patient; while it may be upsetting to not have sex with your husband, it won't last forever.

Chapter 7: Tips for dealing with the period of pregnancy without stress and with peace of mind.

No one can prepare you for the changes your new child will bring to your life, including your relationship with your husband, as everyone will tell you, and it's true. Most couples first feel closer to one another as they share the excitement and joy of having a new baby. It may seem stressful as the weeks pass and your infant starts to go through unsettling phases, especially as regular external employment, child care, and daily routines resume.

Additionally, the unavoidable lack of sleep during the first three months wears on you and may cause everyone to feel grumpy and disagreeable. Since neither of you has much time to unwind, relationships may become a little tense at this point. Even if your relationship has always been great, this development may be difficult and unanticipated.

Relationship roles change with the birth of your first child, usually more so than you expect. This is connected six weeks before sexual activity. Your partner's body is not only going through many physical changes, but she is also nursing, carrying, hugging, and caring for your baby all day, which could make her sensitive to physical touch due to emotional exhaustion. Simply exercise patience, and all of these feelings will pass. Discussing your feelings and the changes in your relationship could help you both have a deeper understanding of what the other is going through.

Although you are not alone, it is a difficult situation. There are methods to deal with this stage, which most couples go through.

These tips have been useful for couples:

Remind yourself and your spouse that you will survive these first few months as a couple. Although the first three months are challenging, they will soon come to an end. Even if it might not seem like it now, things will improve.

Talk and hear each other out. Find out what each of you is thinking and feeling to prevent the emergence of resentment and hostility.

Recognize that the emotional and interpersonal turmoil you're experiencing is a result of the profound changes you and your partner are going through, including:

becoming a parent, which involves certain adaptations.

Changing the nature of the partnership by becoming parents together.

These two are major changes in one's life. The first three months are especially difficult to adjust to them. Usually, three months into a new job, you start to settle down and adjust.

Talk about your views on parenting. Each of you will have your own thoughts and possibly want to approach some situations differently. This is a great chance to talk about things and understand one another's perspectives.

Have a wealth of parenting knowledge at your disposal. Attend parenting classes, parenting centers, and your local Child and Family Health service. You may also browse and read on the internet, where there are a number of respectable parents and many top-notch websites that can provide advice and information.

Males can occasionally be more pragmatic and goal-oriented. When your partner is exhausted and unable to focus after a challenging day with the pregnancy, you may help by helping to create a flexible schedule, being patient and kind, and helping to maintain a consistent approach.

Get Your Relationship Prepared for a Baby, please.

In addition to your relationship, you'll need to get ready for the birth of the child with regard to your house, finances, and even your pets.

Although the baby you'll be bringing home may seem perfect, you should be aware that your relationship with your husband may be significantly impacted by such a small child. The good news is what? Planning beforehand can greatly increase the durability of your relationship.

In this section, we'll go over the most common relationship roadblocks that new parents encounter and discuss how to avoid them in the future.

The initial threat is becoming accustomed to your new roles.

The Great Mom–Dad Divide is a topic that has been discussed for years. It refers to the difference between men and women's responses to parenthood, with women prioritizing their children while men worry about how to maintain an expanding family. However, the paradigm has greatly changed for modern couples. The mother traditionally takes on a more nurturing role, but in the last 30 years, this perception has changed. Nowadays, parents spend the day in business mode and only transition into parent mode when they come home at night. Despite being worn out, they are supporting one another.

Even if baby-care duties are now more equitably distributed among couples, each of you will still need to adapt to your new role as a parent and determine how you'll work as a team.

What could you do to stop it?

What functions best when parents wish to split parenting duties When a mother offers her son full creative freedom to do things his way, it is called a 50/50 split. letting him exercise parental autonomy. If you think you're the only one who knows how to take care of a baby and you won't let dad participate, you're denying yourself and your spouse of the responsibilities, benefits, and pleasures that come with fair co-parenting.

In households where one parent is a stay-at-home parent and is in charge of the majority of newborn responsibilities, communication is more important than ever. By doing so, expectations are set and both partners are made to feel valued. Give the working parent a "training weekend" so that the stay-at-home parent may unwind while the other takes care of the child. It also gives the working spouse and the child some quality time together while teaching them that staying home with the baby is not a vacation.

Keeping score is the second error.

The most important thing is to make sure that each of your tasks appears to be fairly divided, regardless of whether you and your husband share equal responsibility for baby care. When you're worn out and start to wonder why it always seems to be your turn to change a baby's diaper, it's simple to fall into the scorekeeping trap. Avoid keeping score if you don't want to get caught up in a never-ending, exhausting battle over who had the last bath, went to the gym yesterday, and did the laundry.

What could you do to stop it?

Make a "to-do" list that includes everything that has to be done to maintain a home and care for a baby. Then divide the list in half to equally balance the workload and ensure that no partner feels like they are bearing a greater burden than the other. Developing a plan that enables both of you to take time off is essential because new parents need that time to themselves to deal with the challenges and disappointments of parenting a newborn on a daily basis.

The final trap to avoid is lack of sleep.

Every new parent can attest that losing sleep is the biggest adjustment to having a baby. In severe situations, chronic sleep deprivation can lead to psychosis as well as cognitive and memory impairment. At the very least, it might lead to impatience and arguments.

What could you do to stop it?

In order to avoid becoming walking zombies, agree to divide up the nighttime responsibilities. The fact that both parents are awake at the same time is unacceptable. Instead, think about scheduling your work hours so that one parent may wake up with the baby between 10 p.m. and 2 a.m., and the other can work the 2 a.m. to 6 a.m. shift. If you're nursing, prepare a few feedings in advance.

The fourth mistake to avoid is sexual disconnection.

One of the main sources of stress for new parents is the change in their sexual life. Some women may be so busy with their infants that they aren't even thinking about having sex. Because we are designed to ensure that this child lives, our bodies are alerting us not to become pregnant right away. On the other hand, if there isn't any sex, your sweetheart could feel abandoned or even brokenhearted.

It makes sense that mothers would want to delay having sex after the physical strain of pregnancy and childbirth. However, this isn't always the case. While feeling like an adult outside of the position of mother at one point, some women may crave sex as a release and a way to interact with their partner.

This is a completely normal feeling for parents to experience, and it will pass. It's crucial to focus on fostering and keeping a loving connection in the interim.

What could you do to stop it?

Have a sexually frank discussion before the baby is delivered. It will be difficult to prevent the baby from connecting sex with bedtime after they are born. Use every opportunity to be away from your children, such as early in the morning, during naps, and on weekends when things are a little quieter. Date nights are essential because they allow couples to invest in and maintain their relationships. Keep in mind that proximity does not always equate to sex when you begin slowly.

Grannies versus Grannies is the fifth threat.

Grandparents frequently want to leave a lasting impression on their grandchildren by sharing their customs, values, and interests. A turf violation occurs when a mother-in-law or father-in-law crosses the line. It's challenging to tell Grandma that you're sleep training the baby and that she shouldn't be picked up at night since it can damage your connection. Your husband needs to speak up for his parents, and that's his job.

Your relationship with your in-laws may alter, but there may also be issues because both sets of grandparents now have grandchildren. When it comes to things like who gets to see the baby first, who gets to be in the delivery room, and who gets to be called "Grandma," grandmothers frequently compete for the title of "alpha-grandma."

What could you do to stop it?

Couples must develop a plan for managing their family, including who will be there at Christmas, who will be called when, and who will be in the delivery room. Here, it's crucial that you and your partner establish family boundaries. Your in-laws will cooperate if you maintain a united front. If you don't, stress will start to build up inside of you.

What You Can Do Right Away to Get Ready for the Baby.

Knowing what to expect allows you to discuss issues with your spouse before the stress and pressure of a new baby and an endless stream of well-meaning visitors sets in. Knowing the potential issues that many new parents face is half the battle. By approaching parenting on an equal footing, it is also possible to prevent any problems that may arise prior to the child's birth. Here are some suggestions to help you stay out of postpartum relationship squabbles:

• Recognize that you need to adapt your way of life.

Recognize and discuss the fact that once the child is here, you will have less time for yourself. Consider trading off taking breaks so that you can both rest. Marriage counseling may be very helpful for any couple, especially when their relationship is

about to go through significant changes.
Despite what many people believe, marital
counseling is not a last-ditch effort to patch
up a broken relationship.

• Make advance arrangements for support.

Having a support system in place is
crucial for new parents. "Be proactive
about seeking the support you need as
it's a curative component in postpartum
depression," recommends Mary Baker, LCP, a
family therapist at the Well Marriage Center
in Loudoun County, Virginia. "Mom will
depend on Dad for assistance when the baby
is born, and Dad will be exhausted." Rely
on friends and extended family to supply
evening meals for the first few weeks. If you
have the money, think about hiring a cleaner
for the first three months after your child is
born. These seemingly insignificant actions

go a long way in giving you the time you require to bond with your newborn while also enabling you to take care of your home.

• Talk about your sex life.

When the baby is born, sleep can be the only activity taking place under the blankets. Furthermore, if you and your partner are already aware of the possibility, the eventuality won't be as shocking. Being averse to sex is acceptable. But in these situations, a discussion should be held to avoid making either party feel detested and insignificant. Do you require help bringing up the subject? Some apps, like Enduring, will ask you a series of questions to assess the condition of your relationship before offering suggestions on how to strengthen your ability to communicate and resolve conflicts as well as incorporate daily love rituals.

Chapter 8: Practical ideas on how to manage the first few months of a baby's life.

Finally, your newborn is here. Do you now feel like a father? Do not worry if not. After giving birth, the first few days and weeks can seem strange. But things do get better. This is your chance to prove your value and lend as much assistance as you can if you felt a little left out during pregnancy and childbirth. Your child needs lots of time to get to know his dad!

Baby Blues or a More Serious Issue?

Mom could experience some depression around day three after giving birth. This is completely normal and will go away. She can start crying for no apparent cause or merely feel overburdened by obligation. If she had a difficult pregnancy and was eager to have her body back, seeing that it wasn't "back" yet might have been very upsetting. She can also have a variety of aches and pains. Going to the bathroom or even just performing basic personal hygiene duties can be quite challenging and uncomfortable. Her hormone levels have undergone yet another huge change, which has a significant impact on her mood and physique, on top of everything else. Do your role as a father and try to encourage your partner by offering assistance, complimenting her, and taking pleasure in your newborn.

Postpartum depression, which is likely to develop later if your partner develops it, has nothing to do with these initial baby blues. Being in a black hole is far different than just having "the blues." Some individuals characterize postpartum depression in this manner (PPD). The majority of moms are thought to be affected by the disease; PPD is thought to affect 10 to 15 percent of mothers. Less widely recognized is the fact that three to ten percent of fathers can also experience PPD. There will be serious repercussions if this dangerous condition is ignored.

Recognize the PPD Symptoms

If you or your partner has PPD, being aware of and recognizing some of the symptoms will help you get support for yourself or your relationship. To watch out for are the following signs:

• Panic or anxiety attacks.

• A sense of helplessness.

• Frequent episodes of crying.

• Loss of appetite or energy.

• Loss of delight from your infant or from routine activities.

• Decreased sex desire.

• Shifts in mood.

• The difficulty falling asleep, even when the infant is settled.

• Persistent melancholy with nothing to look forward to.

• Suicidal ideas.

Every situation is unique. Talk to each other about how you're feeling and visit a doctor if you suspect that you or your partner may have PPD.

Helping Others

Supporting your partner if she has PPD may seem impossible, but there are many ways you may contribute. Try a few of these suggestions:

• Set aside some time for the two of you to spend together. Regular "us" time can relieve your stress together and help you find some common ground once more.

• Allow her to speak while you listen, or have her speak with a friend she feels comfortable talking to.

• Assume more responsibility for the baby's care and housework so she can try to sleep. Obtain the assistance of relatives and friends if you are unable to handle everything.

• Reward her with a wonderful present, a romantic evening, or spa treatments.

• Verify that she is keeping up with any necessary therapies, medical appointments, or prescriptions.

Try any of the following suggestions for more PPD support and assistance, if either of you needs it:

• Consult your physician. He can provide a variety of solutions, such as therapy or prescription drugs. He might also be familiar with sources for local support groups.

· Seek out help in your neighborhood; many hospitals host PPD support groups. Online communities can also save your life.

• Engage in some exercise. Feeling healthy and active might improve your mood and your partner's mood. It only takes a little bit of exercise each day—about 30 minutes—to release mood-enhancing chemicals.

• Consult your friends and relatives. You could be surprised at how eager individuals are to assist, and many of them might have gone through similar situations.

It is possible to discover a way to support your partner or yourself during postpartum depression. Think things through and seek assistance if you feel lost.

Regardless of how tense things become, make sure you and your partner have effective communication. To make sure you are on the same page when it comes to feeding the baby, changing diapers, and establishing a routine, check in frequently. Ask her how she feels about going back to work, if that was her plan, and be there to support her if she needs to express her erratic feelings. Above all else, keeping the lines of communication open will help you and your partner stay connected and function as a team as you both experience the unknowns of new parenthood.

Chapter Nine

Chapter 9: Take care of yourself for fathers, to stay mentally and physically fit, and to communicate easily with your partner

The following suggestions will help you prepare for fatherhood and address bigger issues:

1. Do some reading and investigation.

Up until recently, the quantity of pregnancy and early motherhood books available spoke primarily from the perspective of the woman, but dad books are becoming more common.

So read as much as you can to help you on your journey.

2. Get involved in the pregnancy.

Spend time and effort on the pregnancy, be curious about the procedure, and discuss it with your partner. The first few days are critical because they set the tone for your level of involvement and interest once your child is here. Every stage of development is filled with wonder and amazing advancement. Being attentive, observant, involved, and nurturing are all positive behaviors.

Attend as many doctor's appointments as you can, especially the one where you first hear the baby's heartbeat. Ask about the development of your unborn child and the stages of pregnancy. Talk about birth preparation, different delivery options, how to pack a hospital bag, and how to cradle a baby. Take advantage of the chance to bond with your partner and your unborn child by taking pleasure in the process.

3. Consider working with a therapist or coach.

Your childhood will almost probably have an impact on how you behave as a parent, regardless of whether you had a wonderful relationship with your father or there was space for improvement. Father of two young children and well-known YouTuber with a fatherhood-focused audience, La Guardia Cross, asserts that "fatherhood, like any relationship, is a mirror, and your baggage will be exposed." "You'll be able to get through it, so don't be concerned. It's okay that some of your baggage will remain hidden until you have children. As a father, you have the opportunity to develop."

Whether your childhood was difficult or unclear or if the thought of parenting simply makes you nervous, know that you are not alone in having an emotional reaction to the notion of doing so. Before the baby is born, it's a good idea to acknowledge and process these emotions. It may be helpful to work with a therapist who can assist you in deconstructing your experiences (past and present) and creating healthy coping mechanisms to handle the stress and issues that come with fatherhood.

4. Visualize being the father you want to be.

It's simple to think that you'll never be a better father than your favorite sitcom parent or your fatherly role model. Spend some time telling yourself that you'll make a great father in your own special way. Think about what that might mean for you. What sort of pursuits do you pursue? Where do you spend your time with your child (ren)? What are a few things that you would never want to miss?

If these ideas fail, try seeing your child as an adult. What do you wish others would recall about you? Focus on the guidance and love you want to provide, as well as the teachings you want to impart. Think about how your roles might compliment one another and how yours and your spouse's do.

Examining the various parenting philosophies out there and deciding which ones you prefer is perhaps good.

5. Create a financial strategy.

It's a good idea to reassess your spending early in pregnancy. The expectant partner can be worried about losing their income, having to pay for medical expenses, and weighing the possibility of taking paid or unpaid parental leave. Fathers can help to stabilize the family's finances by planning ahead.

Get your finances in order, set up automatic bill payments, settle any unpaid debts, and, if at all feasible, attempt to get a few months ahead. How? This can entail applying for loan forgiveness, consolidating debt, or proactively finding out about work benefits that might be especially advantageous. Do everything you can to make your financial situation less stressful because being a parent entails a plethora of new expenses.

6. Establish a family budget.

Together with your partner, calculate the cost of parenting and establish a family budget. overestimate the price of everything, including child care, lactation specialists, and a crib that complies with safety regulations. All of these products fall within a reasonable price range, but your budget should cover high-end purchases so you can access professional assistance when you need it. Any extra cash can be used to pay for future costs like dental work, college or trade school, family vacations, and so forth.

7. Preparing meals.

As much food as you can prepare and store in advance should be done so that no one needs to worry about cooking during the frantic days after birth. Get recipe books like The First Forty Days if you enjoy cooking so you can prepare nutritious meals for your family (especially for the nursing parent). When family members and friends inquire about how they can help, request one or two home-cooked meals. The healthiest delivery alternatives should be gathered and kept in a safe, easily accessible location. Put them on your phone's fast dial for even greater results.

8. Invest in a car seat.

Your most important after-birth item may be a good infant car seat because you cannot leave the hospital without one. Learn how to utilize it and how the bucket seat is attached to the base before you need it. Others are secured by a regular seat belt, while some are held in place by hooks between the seats. In any event, installing a car seat is harder than it first appears. Read all of the instructions and get everything in the car with plenty of time to spare to be prepared.

9. Prepare the baby's room.

It could be difficult to choose nursery furniture because everything is so adorable. Choose anything, even if you think you'll change your mind afterwards. Don't wait until the last minute to paint the walls. The nursery should be free of paint odors prior to the arrival of the infant. The crib, changing table, and dresser are just a few examples of the necessary furniture that can be built or bought. You shouldn't use a hammer or screws if you're sleep deprived and have hazy vision. Although you will have a few months after the baby is born to baby-proof the house, it is always a good idea to complete any tasks that can be completed before the baby is born.

10. Finish any significant projects you are presently working on.

Likewise, finish any unfinished business, especially significant ones at work. Try to finish them or assign someone who can finish them without you. There is parental guilt. It's the idea that you should be spending time with your kids when you're doing anything else that looks more important, like going to work, working on side projects with friends, or pursuing prior interests. Try to accomplish optional tasks or let everyone know in advance that you'll be taking a vacation to avoid feeling bad. When your spouse and child require time and attention that was previously dedicated to anything else, lowering your expectations can help you feel less stressed.

Chapter 10: How to turn this period into one of the most beautiful in your life and not a time of stress and confusion.

Now that your partner's pregnancy is done, you two are getting ready for the first few months you will spend at home with your newborn. This is a wonderful period of change, love, and admiration. As you both embrace motherhood and develop together, you will see a beautiful development in both yourself and your partner. The best ways to change a baby's diaper, how to properly handle a baby, and whether to look into local Mommy & Me or baby support groups in your region are all things that you and your spouse should learn. You and your partner can better understand how to care for your own child by interacting with other families who have young children. This entails baby-proofing, viewing endless web tutorials, and learning the hard way by making error after error. After all, the road to motherhood won't be free of difficulty, blunders, or difficulties. You will be able to manage the first few months of your baby's life, nevertheless, if you collaborate with your partner, loved ones, and close friends.

Interacting with Your Baby at Home:

There might not be anything more delightful than bringing your new baby inside for the first time. However, you might experience a range of feelings. Nervousness and anxiety are nothing new for new fathers. The lack of control you experience as a result of being unable to unwind on the couch without first tending to your infant may really make you feel afraid.

Coming home, however, is a wonderful opportunity to begin building a bond with your infant. Since your partner was likely performing the most of the feeding and snuggling with your child, you might not have spent a lot of time with them when they were in the hospital. Now it's your turn to consider how to hold, adore, and develop a relationship with them. Typically, newborns don't do much. They primarily eat, sleep, and urinate. Do not allow that prevent you from making an effort to connect.

Starting a baby/father routine in which you spend time with your child by using skin-to-skin contact can be something you want to think about. Along with singing and talking, you can take walks with your kid.

It's time to unwind after doing some baby-proofing and getting ready for your child. Put your infant in their cot or bassinet, then go to bed or watch TV. Your newborn baby's temperament and attitudes should be your primary focus as you learn to live with them. Consider this period as learning time rather than being frustrated by the activities you can no longer accomplish. Get familiar with your baby and their environment by spending time with them in the nursery.

Other suggestions include rocking your infant to soothing music, singing lullabies, pulling hilarious faces at them, or allowing them to spend time on their stomachs when they can support their head and neck. Remember that reading to your child and talking to them both help to activate their brains.

How to Rock and Hold Your Baby

It's quite acceptable for you to experience a healthy amount of anxiety as a new parent over how to hold and rock your child to sleep. Holding this small baby in your arms can be a terrifying experience. You will, however, become accustomed to it with time and experience. Here is a brief summary of the most crucial points to keep in mind before picking up, holding, or cradling your infant.

● When you initially lift up your baby, support their head with your palm and take special care not to hit their fragile skull at the top. The areas between the skull's bones where incomplete bone growth occurs are known as fontanels ("Video: Baby's Soft Spots," 2020). Your kid will be able to exit the delivery canal more easily because to these soft regions.

Slide one hand under your infant's head and neck while using the other to support their bottom when removing them from the crib or cot. When you feel comfortable holding your child, you can pick them up and cradle them against your chest.

After picking up your infant, lay their head against your chest and brace their neck by sliding your hand up from the bottom of your child. Put your other hand under your baby's bottom and then move your baby's head to the crook of your elbow. With this cradle hold, your infant will be entirely supported in your arms.

● When burping your infant, you'll also need to be familiar with the shoulder hold. As a result, you will hold your baby's neck and head with your hand while allowing them to rest on your chest and shoulder. To keep your baby supported, put your other hand under their bottom. When you burp, you should be sitting comfortably and leaning slightly backward so that your baby is snuggled against your chest and you can stroke their back with the hand that would have been holding their neck to encourage burps to come out.

● It is never a good idea to hold a hot drink, a hot pan, or a knife with one hand while holding your baby in the other. Never have a drink or prepare food before putting your infant in the bassinet or cot.

● Gently rocking your baby to sleep is a highly popular method for achieving this. When your baby is in the cradle hold, you often achieve this by swaying at the hips. You might also pace or stroll gently. As they go off to sleep, some parents like to take their babies on a tour around the house and get them acquainted with the surroundings.

You may occasionally feel frightened when holding your baby and fear dropping the infant, but this is unlikely to happen. It just takes some getting used to having their tiny body in your arms.

How to Bathe Your Child

Many fathers will experience moments of terror during the beginning of a diaper change, especially because you might be reluctant to bend or move your baby's legs in certain directions. You'll doubt if you're harming them or whether they should be bending in that direction about a hundred times, but you must have faith in yourself. If your infant is uncomfortable, they will cry and complain. The procedure for changing a diaper is straightforward:

1. If you're not at home, place your infant on a flat surface or the changing table.

2. Take off your baby's pants or unbutton their onesie.

3. Remove the diaper's little plastic velcro tabs.

4. Check the extent of the diaper change your infant needs by opening the diaper. You could need just one wipe, but you'll probably need a lot.

5. Clean your infant's diaper region thoroughly to remove any remaining poop or urine. Make sure to look at their back. Large amounts of excrement may occasionally ascend their back rather than remain in the diaper.

Apply baby powder to prevent chaffing at 6.

7. Lift your baby's bottom half once they've been cleaned, then put a diaper beneath their torso.

8. Pull the diaper in between their legs, then reattach the little velcro tabs.

9. If your baby's onesie and pants are dirty, put them in a fresh set; if they are clean, re-clasp or replace the old ones.

Check that out! You just performed an independent diaper change.

Chapter 11: Find information on issues big and small -how to Learn how to thrive as new parents with helpful tips on everything from bottle temperature to father's bonding with the new baby.

Many new parents have to deal with various arguments. These are immeasurable, and every time you think you've figured one out, another one pops up. Just a handful of the discussions you'll have throughout your child's first few months of life are on the list below:

When should we stop breastfeeding? The most natural way to feed your child is by nursing, and most pediatricians advise doing so exclusively for at least six months before starting to introduce other foods to one-year-olds and older alongside breastmilk ("What Are The Benefits," 2021). Both mother and child gain several advantages from breastfeeding. Your child's chance of developing asthma, obesity, diabetes, and respiratory illnesses is decreased by breastfeeding. By having fewer risks for breast cancer, ovarian cancer, diabetes, and high blood pressure, your partner can gain from nursing. Nevertheless, some mothers choose to continue breastfeeding for up to two years. However, if breastfeeding is too difficult for your partner or has negative affects, there is no guilt in choosing formula. It's understandable that some women choose not to breastfeed, and there is nothing wrong with encouraging your spouse in their decision.

Pets and newborns. It is completely normal to experience some trepidation when bringing your brand-new infant to your possibly raucous and animated animals. In fact, once a baby enters the house, life with your dogs will alter. According to a survey of over 600 dog and cat owners that was presented at the 2010 American Sociological Association convention, pet owners who have children spend less time with their animals (Fields, n.d.). Even while this could be discouraging, having kids and pets comes with its share of responsibilities. Instead of focusing on the time you won't spend with your pet, you could want to encourage a warm and sincere bond between your child and your pet so that they can have the same kind of relationship that you and your cat do.

● In light of this, you should get your pets ready to welcome your child into the house. To assist them acquire accustomed to the sound of a baby screaming or laughing, try introducing them to the lotions you intend to use for your infant and playing kid noises from online videos. Pets can become anxious by sudden changes, so give them a tour of the nursery so they can get used to the new furniture placement.

● I'll let them cry it out. Some outdated recommendations may suggest letting a crying newborn "cry it out" and that crying helps a baby's lungs. Allowing your child to cry at night is frequently mistaken for sleep training, but there are many more approaches that don't entail ignoring your child's cries for affection, warmth, and attention. Each family will have a different period of time that you and your partner stay gone during the sleep training process to help your child learn that you will return for them. When you use the cry-it-out technique, you merely disappear, and your child can get concerned that you won't ever return. Additionally, excessive weeping, fussing, and demanding are unnecessary throughout the sleep-training process. Many strategies employ kinder techniques. Finding a sleep training technique that works for your family is key.

Remember that sleep training is a continuous process that takes time, patience, and effort. After just one round of sleep training, you cannot expect to be finished. Your youngster could occasionally relapse and require retraining. This is typical and to be anticipated.

Long-term independence for your child can be fostered through sleep training. Your life will be simpler, your sleep will improve, and your child's self-confidence will rise when they are capable of managing their own sleep and are able to self-soothe sufficiently to do so on their own.

Entertainment for infants

As was previously indicated, until they are old enough for tummy time, newborns lead somewhat inactive lives. They should begin tummy time about four months, when they can support their own head, but until then, they will probably just like to look around, play with small rattles or teethers, and observe their parents. Small, sturdy mirrors for a crib or stroller may keep babies entertained for hours. Additionally, contrasting-colored scarves and music might enhance their senses (just remember to never leave them unsupervised with the scarf). As long as you're careful with them, you could even want to have them move their limbs to the music to help them comprehend beats and noises better.

A diaper-change trade. It can be challenging to decide who should get up in the middle of the night to change the baby's diaper, particularly if you and your partner are both worn out. By establishing who will manage which nights and adhering to that timetable, taking turns can help alleviate this problem. Depending on how worn out one of you is from the day, you and your spouse might occasionally have to switch things up, and that's good. You two will manage diaper changes just well as long as the labor is divided.

Is it typical for infants to vomit milk? Yes. Although you might feel frightened when it happens, it's quite natural and acceptable for your baby to burp up some milk after a meal. In the event that this occurs, don't panic. Move on with your day after wiping your kid down with a towel or burp cloth. If your child exhibits other signs of something else, such as a temperature or discomfort, think about bringing him to the pediatrician or phoning the nurse for guidance.

Crib vs. bassinet. Due to its lower size and portability, a bassinet is frequently chosen by new parents over a crib. A bassinet won't be big enough for your kid to fit in throughout the toddler stage, but a crib will be big enough for them as they develop. Both are suitable for your baby's development and sleep. which is most secure? Have both and get rid of the bassinet once your child can turn over or sit up.

Development of a Baby: The First Year

Because you might visit your pediatrician frequently, it might as well be your home away from home. You'll be coming in for additional vaccinations, checks, and other issues like horrible diaper rashes or sensitive skin every few months. Your child will really have six wellness appointments over the first year at the following ages:

Months One through Twelve: Month One, Month Two, Month Four, Month Six, Month Nine, and Month Twelve.

These visits are standard, and the doctor will weigh your infant, measure their length, and perform a full physical during them. The pediatrician will assess your child's reflexes, listen to their heart and lungs, check their eyes, ears, and mouth, listen to their heart and lungs, check their eyes, ears, and mouth, check their eyes, ears, and mouth, assess the soft spots on your infant's head and make sure the shape of their head is within normal limits, assess any jaundiced skin, look for rashes, and check for birthmarks, assess your child's belly and the umbilical cord Additionally, pediatricians will be checking to see if a boy's testes have "descended into the scrotum" (Beer, 2019). Additionally, they will check the healing of any circumcision treatments. The pediatrician will then move your infant's hips and legs to check their range of motion.

The administration of any immunizations that are due at that time. You may find this unsettling since you don't want to witness your child suffering. However, these shots and immunizations will shield your child from much graver illnesses. Typically, a parent will hold the baby throughout the injections to provide them with all the care and comfort they need.

You can get any questions you have during the exam answered. Don't be afraid to express any worries. Keep in mind that your child's pediatrician has likely seen it all, so don't be afraid to ask questions. Remember that many pediatrician offices will have a helpline you can call if a problem arises. For instance, a solution to any rashes, bumps, or worries can be found in only a few minutes. You can get advice from the practice's nurse or doctor about the best medical course of treatment for your child.

Chapter Eleven

Chapter 11: What housework the man should be involved in during the stages of his partner's pregnancy.

Every infant is unique, just as every family is. You'll learn how to read and care for your infant in the next days, weeks, and months in a way that no one else ever will, aside from mom, of course. Use this opportunity to put all the baby care instruction you have received into action. It will involve a lot of trial and error. There is no such thing as a perfect parent, so don't worry. Everyone has done a ton of stupid parenting blunders, especially in the beginning, and their kids have still lived and thrived.

Helping your partner as much as you can is the most important thing you can do. Particularly if she has a cesarean delivery, she will likely be worn out and hormonal for days or even weeks following the birth. So, you'll still have to do the bulk of the chores around the house without complaining. She will need a lot of time to recover before she can resume her pre-pregnancy activities.

If you are feeding your kid via bottle, you can divide the feeding equally, especially at night. One of the best methods to assist the two of you deal with the incredible stress of sleep deprivation you'll face in the first few weeks of motherhood is to take turns nursing the baby. Even if your spouse is nursing, you can still be of great assistance by changing the diaper and seeing to the baby's cleanliness and attire before transferring him to the mother for a feeding.

Making sure mom and the child arrive at planned checkups, preparing meals, and watching out for any well-intended visitors who overstay their welcome are additional ways you may assist. Everyone will be excited to meet your new baby, but your top goal should be to prevent your partner from feeling overburdened and the infant from being disturbed or freaked out by too many visitors. Try to space out guests so that you only see one or two individuals per day, and set aside certain days when you have no visitors so that your new family can get to know one another and unwind.

Chapter Twelve

Conclusion

The next step is to continue honing your talents as an exceptional partner and parent all the way through the years when your child is growing up. Every day will bring forth brand new educational and personal growth possibilities. Having a father like you ensures that life will never again become routine. You are about to set off on an adventure that will live long in the memory. You have already demonstrated that you are dedicated to supporting your spouse totally throughout pregnancy, labor, and delivery; therefore, it is likely that you are going to be an excellent parent to your child. You have shown that you are willing to improve yourself, showing compassion for the needs of your partner and child, and prioritize meeting their requirements, regardless of the difficulties that life may present to your family. Men like you serve as an example for other fathers and men who would like to become fathers. If more partners were to take the effort that you have, then pregnant women all over the world would have happier, healthier, and less stressful pregnancies.

If you found the information in this book to be helpful for your own experience, consider giving it to friends and family members who are also expecting their first child at the same time as you. They will be thankful for your help in teaching them how to put themselves in the shoes of their partners and have a better knowledge of pregnancy.